Stairway to Heaven

ALSO BY ALISON HAWTHORNE DEMING

POETRY

ROPE

GENIUS LOCI

THE MONARCHS: A POEM SEQUENCE

SCIENCE AND OTHER POEMS

POETRY OF THE AMERICAN WEST (EDITOR)

NONFICTION

ZOOLOGIES: ON ANIMALS AND THE HUMAN SPIRIT

THE COLORS OF NATURE: CULTURE, IDENTITY, AND THE
    NATURAL WORLD (COEDITOR)

ANATOMY OF DESIRE: THE MOTHER/DAUGHTER SESSIONS (COAUTHOR)

WRITING THE SACRED INTO THE REAL

THE EDGES OF THE CIVILIZED WORLD: A JOURNEY IN NATURE
    AND CULTURE

GIRLS IN THE JUNGLE

THE COLORS OF NATURE (COEDITOR)

TEMPORARY HOMELANDS

Stairway to Heaven

ALISON
HAWTHORNE
DEMING

PENGUIN POETS

PENGUIN BOOKS
An imprint of Penguin Random House LLC
375 Hudson Street
New York, New York 10014
penguin.com

LIBRARY OF CONGRESS CATALOGING-IN-PUBLICATION DATA
Names: Deming, Alison Hawthorne, 1946– author.
Title: Stairway to heaven / Alison Deming.
Description: New York, NY : Penguin Books, [2016] | Series: Penguin poets
Identifiers: LCCN 2016022176 (print) | LCCN 2016027464 (ebook) |
ISBN 9780143108856 (paperback) | ISBN 9781101992128 (ebook)
Subjects: | BISAC: POETRY / American / General.
Classification: LCC PS3554.E474 A6 2016 (print) | LCC PS3554.E474 (ebook) |
DDC 811/.54—dc23

Printed in the United States of America
1   3   5   7   9   10   8   6   4   2

Set in Bembo Std
Designed by Ginger Legato

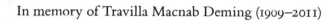

In memory of Travilla Macnab Deming (1909–2011)

and Rodney Macnab Deming (1944–2011)

CONTENTS

STAIRWAY TO HEAVEN

The idea came to me in the kitchen
while I was cutting cilantro for the black beans
and my friend and I were talking
while the sea outside remained the sea
holding its mysteries in the dark
tempting us with its surface dazzle.
The idea came as if a theory of war
I'd been working on though
in truth it just bubbled up like
the first disturbance in a pot
that means the soup is about to boil.
Is there something in us, I asked him,
my friend who was waving the celery tops
at me and asking with his eyes
if they belonged in the soup and
I was saying yes with my eyebrows
and by "us" I didn't mean the man and woman
feeling the man-and-woman thing while cooking
together in the kitchen by the sea
where the wind carried salt into our every breath
but I meant our animal selves, our
mysteries-in-the-dark of mind and body
that doesn't feel balanced without
the threat of dangerous animals,
the African brain of us, the sinew
and blood longing for the bond
between predator and prey that we've
tossed with the entrails
of farm-raised salmon and beef.
Mine was an amateur theory of war—
that we wage it—not our kind?
so it's fine to kill them?—

mindless of the mechanism
ticking and cranking and blowing up
beneath the surface inside us.
We don't even know what we're
doing when we do it. What lesson
in being human did we not first learn
from the animals? The cheetah was
the first domestic cat. In ancient Egypt
the keepers asked, as we ask, can we please
make the violent lie down and
go to sleep and when it wakes
to lap calmly from the saucer?
And then the something
that was in us was soup,
a liquor that had blown
from the sea right into our bowls.

Once I had a cat who studied himself
in the mirror. He didn't know
what it was in there staring back at him
but he couldn't stop looking
because the face never turned away
and eyes meeting eyes
want more seeing. It's already dark.
No moonlight. No whip-poor-will—
the bird that tormented my childhood
refusing to take on the night
without incessant song. That bird
must have been the size of a fire hydrant
I thought then but learned later it was
just a pip of feathered life with a voice
insistent as the news, that continuity
of disaster and argument to which
we all belong—bomb in recruiting office,
stoning in public square, crude oil
in everyone's hair, to mosque or not
to mosque. Don't turn away. It's just
the brute world that will outlive us,
the lean hard muscle of it
flexing. But the birds
don't belong, they are settling
into the night, their feathered quilts
ready-made. Some of them
are rising out of their bodies, whole
categories of bodies, and into
the being of non-being where of course
we're all headed after a few more parties
and fixations of eyes upon eyes. But first
who doesn't want to make something

of it, the clutch of childhood's
solitary rages and the way the face
begins to cave in on itself with age
so that it looks like an Arizona landscape,
all contour and defile, telling the outcome
of its story to everyone, leaving out
a few details, so that a person might stare at
himself and say, Don't I know you from
somewhere? You look so familiar and yet . . .

—for Don Bachardy

■ THE TOOTHBRUSH

I'm trying to remember you without nostalgia
thieving your words and hoarding them
because all that I'm getting is the toothbrush
you carried in a mug every day
down the corridor heading for the men's room
to commit a small act of resistance
against breakdown.

                   I always laughed:
you have the best hygiene of anyone
in the department, which was a joke
because the stink of cigarettes
surrounded you like the fry oil
of a prep cook. Still something like
tenderness inhered in the mug
and its rigid little daisy.

Here's how we met: me on job interview
fresh from New England trying
not to sweat in desert heat,
you after friendly dinner with Gail
and studio tour and poetry talk
driving me downtown in some big junk car
with no AC saying Barrio Hollywood
and Hotel Congress and the Shanty.

Then came the test: the story about a whore
in Nogales who had a spider web
tattooed around her pussy. I'm sure that
was the word—offense was the point
and I understood implicit was the question
does your poetry trump your politics?

This was in those years when women
were correcting men as if sex
were a policy that could be rewritten
in a pencil stroke. I passed, laughing it off:
Oh my god you're kidding that's incredible.
A poet can find wonder anywhere
and I did wonder how strong a woman
had to be to take that kind of pain.

Here's how we said good-bye: I came
to visit you, the nurse recalibrating
your drip as you asked, have I got any time?
And you, thumbs down, facing it.
I saw you catch your breath
hand to throat beneath the black t-shirt,
some event the hand would contain,
some moment of self-consolation,
like air was alien.

                    Aurelie called it
the weird majesty of death
that had come over all of us,
people gathering
in a circle, each face
reorganizing itself through
the eyes of another's grief
as if to be animated
were to violate the pure encroachment
of the inanimate.

                    There was a kiss,
me walking you to the bathroom
and then to bed where you lay
in shuttered afternoon light,
others in the room and

you seemed nothing but
this invitation to tenderness.

And what kiss was this—not familial peck,
not lovers' open-mouthed encroachment,
not parental seal of approval but
the mouth opened by the final
so quiet need to say
there is nothing between us
that needs to be cleaned away.

—*for Steve Orlen*
(1942–2010)

The queen grows fat beneath my house
while drones infest the walls

reconnaissance to feed her glut,
wood ripped from studs and joists.

I'll pay to drill the slab and ruin
her pestilential nest. How to find

the song in this day's summons?
I've been accused of darkness

by my inner light. My brother sits
in the chemo chair another long day

of toxic infusion, the house of his body—
bones, brain and balls gone skeltering.

I sit in my parked car listening
to Robert Plant recall how the English

envied the Americans for getting
the blues, getting all of it, into song.

I remember the dream where
brother and sister, adult and equal,

lean and white as lilies, as bare,
dove into a mountain lake, black water,

high elevation, fir trees growing
in flood water that had joined

two lakes into one. Do you ever dream
of animals, I ask him, hospice bed

looking out on a plywood squirrel
perched on cement block wall.

Frequently. A lilt of surprising joy. What kind?
Mostly the jungle animals. Then: I'm going

to do my exercises now. What exercises?
I like pacing, he said, immobilized

upon his death nest of nine pillows.
Then he closed his eyes to become the inward one

whose only work was to wear a pathway
back and forth within his enclosure.

I found an old cartoon my brother drew, our mother keeping
the folded yellow second sheets, *Mementoes which mean a great deal to me*, their
pencil lines smudged, the paper scented
with pencil shavings, lead and cigarette ash, bodies
for both of them now things of the past in
which they no longer labor or love or linger over the
details of family history as I do trying to center
myself in their absence and love them without taint of
anger or judgment or regret, just carry the
sense of them a little further down the hall
that leads away from the rooms in which they died as
if the cartoon might be what they
need in the afterlife I'm making for them in this walk
down the page. Hello, my brother, come down
to me from heaven or up from hell, the
difference is nothing but a hysterical
joke once you've drawn your dark cartoon of a pool-hall,
Christ, *Joe and Mary*, hot rodding toward Bethlehem—they
look in vain at motel and bar and *Dirty Eddie's Gas* for someone to allow
them refuge—*and Mary was eight months gone*. Their
flight from *Governor Graft* must say something lovely
about you as a teenager wounded into darkness, a boy who skirts
the edge of disaster by morphing *Gov. Graft* into *Dirty Eddie* (to
note here same toothy grin of greed on both, cigar in teeth, men who graze
on poison and make a deal the desperate can't refuse). The nativity, no
story our mother believed, but art for her meant the captive's flight over the wall.

—*a golden shovel after Gwendolyn Brooks*

In the cutter's house   no Proustian
goodnight kiss   drew him
to its warmth.   Curt, dutiful,
a peck as when   a dove stabs
one millet seed   only one when
the ground lies scattered   thick with feed.
Sometimes a razor   sometimes the coal
of a lit cigarette   echo of father's
bedtime lightshow   the orange tip
swirled in the dark   father invisible
but magic   a thrill you couldn't see
when the lights   turned on.
But his wounds were   no entertainment
this act that left his arm   a cratered row of scars
rough edged rounds   of cigarette tip
as if some small fossils   had been eroded
from his flesh.   Once he carved initials
of a girlfriend   into his forearm
to prove his love   could stand up to his pain.
No. Some need   to stoke endorphins
as new science would   propose some brains
have chemistry   that's incomplete
without some risk   to spike them
into fluency   neurotransmitters
an easy pour   at this barroom in the skull.
Thinking this way   makes it easier
to love   harder to be angry as
say at a person   born with a club foot
because his gait looks odd   harder to judge
the cruelties   when it's possible
he had no choice   but to be what he was.
No one who loved him   could ever get close enough

to what he suffered   though he would never
say he suffered   suffering being
so close to what he was   this pain he never could snuff
though he spent his life   in devotion to
chemical assistance   heroic in his outlaw
hipster way   his pain now mine
that must   be written down
to expel it   from his ghost.
Shy ghost   my new friend
and old adversary   hangs around outside
my door not sure   where he belongs.
Come in   leave your green eyes
that glow in the dark   outside
and come in   to this house of
your failures and mine   a kiss
dear brother   now, sleep.

Someone is making love this afternoon.
Why not when the sun has broken
through the low pressure that had
everyone in a lustless sulk for weeks
and now that electric blue sky
buzzes in the brain and makes
the heat rise. Even those who are not
making love are thinking of someone
who called them my darling or my plum
as I do remembering how he would harden
against my back in the morning
and I would turn to him.

Someone is being tortured this afternoon
by his own body as disease
flares into encampments along
the river of his spine. He feels
their fires burning and prays
as a soldier does the night before battle.
He is growing porous from the fight,
his eyes becoming wide and guileless.
A strange and gentle kindness has come over him
as if he is wandering in a mysterious place
and wants to be especially polite
to the locals feeling he is a foreigner there.

Someone is out on the streets this afternoon.
Town beach packed with bikinis
and volleyball and a dog wearing
a sunhat who rides in a convertible.
Someone is everyone out for the pleasures
of a town with a disk jockey pumping

up the beach crowd into salutes to the sun
and living in a body and the day all suffused
with the finest gold pollen that keeps falling
and falling onto our glasses and iPhones and windshields
and into our lungs, matter made spirit,
meaning the breath and what's deepest in us.

—*for Rodney Deming*
(1944–2011)

White bone faces, eye
sockets black vined with roses
so red they declare
amnesty with death. I'm here
for my mother and brother.

Street vendor paints me
a mourner in white face, mold
green eyes, rusted cheeks
yellow marigold blooming
from the round bulb of my chin.

Princess with lace-up
green velvet bustier and
mink stole. Whose look? Whose
mink? I'm thinking dead mother,
lips sealed with painted sutures

Faux Indian chief
wears headdress, feathers silvered
and splayed like Aztec priest come
back to see what's become of
death in our time. So have I.

Remember the stage
makeup kit our parents kept
in their clothes closet?
Pancake, rouge, and mineral
spirits? Braids of human hair

to unravel and
comb for making beards, then white
shoe polish to make
them old? So easy to be
transformed. Now this. You, too. Gone.

Another corpse lies
in his pine coffin playing
the concertina
while pallbearers skate him down
Fourth Ave to the finale.

Who's in the parade
and who's out? How can you tell?
Where do I register?
Oh, you don't have to sign up.
We're all in this parade.

The sad thing is I
can't see my own face. What bones
and flowers I wear.
Who knows what person's hiding
beneath the angel suit, bling

wings bigger than the
walking angel's body. May
she rise. X-rays not
required. Day of the Dead
everyone's bones are showing.

■ THE COMPLEX

Crumpled wad tied with dirty twine
homeless person's treasure
lead cladding and nothing inside
but more lead—the weight makes you
want to drop to your knees
but its poison makes you
fight the enemy who's invisible
or never was there only
the one and only
package of grief.
A parasite starts out small
but grows in the gut.
A conversation
you can't stop having
with a person who isn't there,
fighting back the words
when the person is there.
This argument, tense,
interior, impossible to quiet
like the backdrop on a stage
always there setting the tone.
The work is knowing
the difference between
the complex owning you
and you owning the complex.

shoulder heavy bison   cascade of running horses
trill of rhino horns   dance as a book of stills
made motion picture   as pages flip
vulva coaled on pendulous rock   these are the inner life
its demands   on the human hand   that made
the early mind   find time   for virtuosity   hard won   then as now
by quarry in a lightless place   where bears had marked
rock walls while sharpening claws   so art found shelter there
repeating the animal's movements   but clawless and thinking
I am that   and I am not that   the animal
a self-willed power   in the mind   that contains
something the artist hungers for   a self-willed world within
that disrupts   where the mind   thought it was going
something unsettling   that moves the line   so the inner can be seen

tight scrotum of the maneless lion   flared nostril of the horse in flight
exertions of the body   the maker   reaching full height
to press palm against stone   choosing the flawed hand
to represent the self   little finger bent from injury
red prints set in a grid   wonder that the hand
can sing   other hands come   five thousand years
of overlapping lines   that don't conflict   with what
came before   but honor   the whole stampede
bison aurochs mammoth   in flight out of the silent dark
forty thousand years   from then to now   and still
the ceiling drips calcite   slow art   coating the cave floor
the mindless stone accreting   on what life   had left in the cavern
before a landslide sealed it   bear skull laved   with milky sheen
turned solid   and bright   as new white porcelain

—after Werner Herzog

We know the desert has consciousness because the saguaros
    stand up and speak as one about the heat.

They tell the Gila woodpeckers to come in out of the sun.
    They tell a man or a woman lost without water to lie

in the column of shade they make out of their kindness.
    The saguaros all hum together like Tibetan or Gregorian monks

one green chord that people hear when they drive
    through Gates Pass and come to the place where they gasp.

Beauty does that though the nihilist will make an ironic joke
    about the note of surprise that has escaped

from his or her loneliness. The smile from the joke will cover
    for the smile for joy. That's okay. Consciousness

is like the saguaro's decision to wait half a century to come up
    with arms though arms were in its mind all along.

■ QUESTIONS FOR A SAGUARO

Not that I want to be a god or a hero. Just to change into
a tree, grow for ages, not hurt anyone.

—CZESLAW MILOSZ

If it takes you a hundred years
to grow your first arm
for how long do you feel
the sensation of
craving something new?

Did you ever feel impatient
those years after someone
put his shirt over your head
and even with spines
cutting through denim
it took decades to grow
your way out of confinement?

Does it feel like gorging or
fate when rain
comes and you suck up
every drop as fast as you can
even if you starve the palo verde
that sheltered your youth?

Sometimes people are thrilled
to see you lined up
in disarray like soldiers
off-duty forever in the quiet desert.
Does anything thrill you?
A mountain lion scratching
its backside on your spines?
Flowers erupting from your head?

Fruit loaded with seeds will
move all you've learned
from your one rooted spot
into new places called the future.
Does it mean for you joy
or unburdening when those
sweet packages
fall to the ground?

One
white winged
dove at dawn
pecking bugs out of
the noisy crown of royal palm.

Cold
wet rot
bark made from
remnant fronds broken
at the ready wrench of a hand.

Not
hand–like
the stance more
lollipop, stop sign,
sentry line, erect as GIs.

Palm
at end
of the mind:
are its birds silent
as night—or dawn, city in flight?

Fronds
pre–dawn
menace, fist
of machetes raised
against metallic sky. Come, sun.

There's
nothing
much to say
re being a tree—
simple-minded master of dirt.

Dis-
tiller
of sugar,
bowing to mean storms,
repeater of formal gesture.

What
the palm
might need to
borrow a mind for:
saying the feel of reach and thirst.

You might call it a river
this track of sand and scrub
that threads through the city
inviting runners, riders, taggers,
lofting gliders, singing coyotes
and a solo cougar. A pueblo of bats
nests under bridge girders
to nurse their young, adapting
their old ways to city life
their sonar touching whatever
comes near, their tongues
licking bugs out of air.
You might call it a river
when the monsoon brings
a flood that bashes
apart the stillness
that threads through the city,
the brown churn hurling
dirt and weeds and shopping carts
until it settles and drops whatever
it has carried there on the spot
where the flowing has stopped. You might
call it a river unless you came
to its banks the summer when
the mountains raged with wildfire
and the National Forest charred.
The rains as they eased
began the healing but it was slow,
runoff threading through
crevice, gully and wash, gathering
in Agua Caliente and Tanque Verde
then filling the Rillito, carrying

blackened silt of wood
and rhizome so fine it made
the racing flow shine black
as liquid coal. I was there,
I saw the river do its work,
how even as it might thirst
for water, might long to break
the paving that impounds
its desire to meander, how even
as the river might be
a stranger to itself,
lost to the city's velocity
and constant subdued roar,
how the river will rise
to the fact of weather
and tell its story of
beauty, damage and loss. You might
call it a river though it looks
nothing like what you imagine
a river to be, water shining
one day black as liquid coal
and next day becoming again
the stillness that threads
through the city where something
you might call your life reveals itself
to be an eddy in the unseen
flow of all that continues.

The white-billed ducks at shoreline paddled off.
The black ones with white flanks stayed put.
I had names for none of the birds paddling the artificial lake
but they had been here long enough for understandings
to emerge between them. Not coot or scaup or eider.
They came after the graders and backhoes had gone,
the shallows stitched with leafy water plants
like miniature taro but I had no name
for them as I had none for the white flowers,
petals wrinkled from the bud stage
smoothing in the sun—like blackberry,
serrated leaf, russet-tinged and caney stalk
though crawling low in grass like untrellised ivy.
None for the tall-stalked weed topped with pea-sized
yellow flowers, perhaps, a version of dandelion
or sunflower, something common, but its name
was not what I wanted rather the accidental hybridizing mess
where vegetation runs to excess then decay, again, again.
I pressed five wildflowers flat in my notebook, carrying them
from the nameless place to one I had known before I came.

Two men in lawn chairs straw hats
royal blue Crocs
cast lines into the gulf.
Great blue heron stands
ten feet behind the men
upright as a deacon
focused on what's beyond.

When the heron grabs its supper
the tinseled energy
pincered and thrashing
crosswise in the bill
the bird takes its time
shifting the fish so it slips
without struggle down the throat.

Does the bird feel the catch
flitter in its belly?
Does that disturb
or arouse or satisfy
the heron? Or is it just fact?
I don't think the deep-sea shrimp
feel much when they gorge

on luminescent bacteria
that light up their gut
making them a neon sign
for food. So it goes all along
the chorus line of appetite
as it goes here. A huge gull stands
ten feet behind the heron

the gull watching the heron
the heron watching the men
the men watching the chalky waves
and me watching them all
feeling something
is being conveyed
I am meant to record

as if to watch and
watching to see
the moment opening
into what continues
as if any moment
were the purpose
any of us had been
called to, this sentience
so here and gone.

The animals do not laugh
except hyenas but they
mean hunger or feasting or
get off my back. The laughter
of animals erupts as
a gesture that ripples through
flanks or freezes head and eye.
For them too the spontaneous
is a means of defense.
Nothing is funny
to animals, pure muscle
more serious than the history
of thought, though I have seen
desert cottontails
dance for joy in the rain.

The hummingbird moth beats its wings
like a helicopter tilting toward the hospital.
The eight-spotted forester sips nectar
from one purple milkweed floret
needling into the folds and tunnels of tissue.
How many days will the flower last and how does
the moth know where to find it? It cannot hear the flower open.
It has no map and no nose. No moon calendar and no *Farmer's Almanac*.
I gather the names of all that swoop and flail and flitter
in the steamy weed horde of a July morning.
The somewhat-musical conehead (formerly known
as the long-beaked conehead) renamed
when someone said I thought I knew it
but then realized I did not. I want to hear
something I have never heard before
so I lie down still as a blade of grass
waiting for the hustle of wingbeats
to mate with summer air.

First came the scouts who felt our sweat in the air
and understood our need to make a sacrifice.

We were so large and burdened with all we had carried
our blood too rich for our own good. They understood

that we could give what they needed and never miss it.
Then came the throng encircling our heads like acoustic haloes

droning with the me-me-me of appetite. We understood
their pleasure to find such hairless beasts so easy to open and drink.

We understood their female ardor to breed and how little
they had to go on considering the protein required to make

their million-fold eggs. Vibrant, available, and hot,
we gave our flesh in selfless service to their future.

—for Peter Cunningham

He wanted to talk, the man from Fish and Game
who had taken time after twelve hours on the road
to observe two bald eagles nesting at the Moosehorn Refuge
where at dawn he would begin five days of fire training.
How do they teach you, set a fire in the woods
and make you put it out? Yeah, he said . . . eventually.
We sipped beers on the veranda while the river bled
pink and silver, glassy smears that marked
how the inflowing tide disrupted the water's seaward pull.
A German couple joined us. They were making
a square dance tour of America, following the guide book
that told them, state by state, each community
where they could find others who knew
the promenade and do-si-do, moves shaped
in a pastoral life then sampled by urban dwellers.
Maybe the first pastoralists played
at being hunter-gatherers, spear
becoming javelin, sledge becoming sled.
They showed us their costumes—
cowboy shirt the color of orange popsicles
tiered floral dress puffy and perfect as a doll's bouffant.
The St. Croix went on bleeding in its quiet confusion
and I excused myself to walk along its bank.
Two boys were fishing, perched on a rock,
casting lines into the near dark. They left
when they saw me coming and I was sorry.
The river threw the soft night back up to the sky
pink bouncing off the surface as if water and air
were dance partners, pink like a bog orchid,
something brief that startles the mind
grown accustomed to the browns and mists of the north.

■ WALKING WITH MICHAEL AND JIM
IN THE BLACKOUT

A woman on the hotel veranda said
how will I get ready for the party
without a hairdryer? Traffic lights
went null, ceaseless traffic
crawled up Ocean Ave
contracts written on the spot
for who would go and who would stop
twelve lanes of orderly improvisation
playing at the pace of who knows what.
Shops closed, accordion gates descended
but the bookstore, sweet cloister,
stayed open. We shopped by flashlight
and charged, such license, without approval
(so apt, Calvino's *Numbers in the Dark*)
bought water at the liquor store
waiting in line until the bouncer
announced our turn. On the street
no news no phone (I wouldn't want to be
in South LA tonight, the bouncer said).
The outage covered three states, no six,
all the way to Mexico. Who knew?
We chose to sit it out on the pier,
Ferris wheel empty after fire ladder
rescues, sunbathers blasé
on beach—did they even know
the power was gone? We read aloud
galleys of the poet laureate, a man who
reinvented the role of public poet
by speaking for rivers, dragonflies,
the state of the planet. We took turns
and made a rule the one reading

had to sit in the middle of our bench.
When we finished the poem that pegged
the problem of our species as
"half-mated longing" carried
from childhood, I got stuck
on the phrase. It seemed to render
each of us irreparably solitary
yet incomplete or maybe it was a call
to put childhood to rest, tuck it in
somewhere safe and move on.
The poems were broken by helicopter
noise. Vipers I called the news crew
whose job it was to show us the worst
when the pixels returned. Come down
with your macro lens and shoot us
perched beside the birds-of-paradise
in love with poetry and friendship
and questions that bring quiet to the day.

—for Michael Silverblatt

When the microburst
tunneled through your stand
of old spruce slamming
trees into a field
of flattened sticks that
looked like the wake of
a meteor strike
tiny birch saplings
survived, too lean to
catch wind as a force
that could snap them.
Foresters call this
kind of event a
disturbance regime
and study how land
reorganizes itself
after fire, flood
or volcano. Days
after Mount St. Helens
obliterated
everything within
an eight-mile circle
lacy rhizome threads
raced to occupy
the empty ash, life
experienced at
taking the violent
as catalyst for
what the ancients called
the taming power of the small.

—for Peter Hoffman

Some week when the roof leaks
and the cat has been carried off
by the fox when my brother's
scans sparkle with lesions
when someone hates me
for the good deed I've done
and it's impossible to sleep or wake up

I will return to the island
to see its blue and lavender rocks
I will stare at the ocean a long time
thinking of the man lost at sea
who clung to a sheet of plywood
after his fishing boat went down
his jeans so heavy with water

his hands so cold with cold
that he had to let go
and go down. Trove of the fishers
lost to the deep, the holy
seabed scattered with wrecks
nothing but bones and boots
laid out on the scuttle ground

after the benthic gleaners have gone,
the sad nets coming up empty
laden with such loss that his people
can only shake their heads
and gear up for another day of work.
Something of their faith
may come to me if I stare

all day at the churn and pull
of fearsome tides, the tweeded
surface of the bay. I'll know
whatever I suffer is small on the scale
of what people are made to live through.
A net of words holds a place together
and those who are broken are lifted home.

—in memory of Seamus Heaney

A peat fire glows endlessly
in every house. At night
the fire is smoored with ash
and in the morning the fire
is dug out and renewed
with breath. When cholera
lands once the dead are
removed whole huts
are burned to the ground.
Men gather in a ritual
of renewal fully snuffing
out the fire then rubbing
sticks to start one anew
the unclean destroyed
a new flame a new life.
No one grudged anyone
anything so long as herring
were about silver as coins.
A woman then thought
no longer of her physical death
but of the spirit of death
spectral under the moon
thought of the spirit of seas
and all their hidden schooling.

—after Neil M. Gunn

1.

during my darkest grief the forest
was like an open sea birch trees
the beacon I used to steady my position

my brain felt at home among
saplings that tangle seeking light
that part of the soul Aristotle thought

we held in common with plants
days and weeks cutting trail
at first moving three feet

through thicket then ten then
deeper into black spruce
bow saw and clippers

slung on my back like
Diana's quiver trying to sense
how the path should rise

past cobble and copse
into high fern meadow
and beyond into balsam fir

towering so high they make
beneath them a living room
of reindeer moss and fungi

woods long worked by men
timbers and fieldstones
oxen-hauled downhill even

the skins of island houses
cloaked with fish scale
of cedar shingles cut here

where hardly a cedar tree
can be seen so fruitful
were those times of building

the Greeks had a way to speak
about depth so that each spring
had a name and history

and a supplicant had a place
to go to beg for wisdom
or healing or a song to make

that part of the soul
held in common with song
feel at home North Head

Seal Cove Dark Harbour
do well for singing but
every place needs its Castalia

where older thought
emerges like steam
from vents in a caldera

2.

the island lies under a pall
of cold rain sea churlish
and aluminum gray

whitecaps slapping
horizon dissolved
no edge just one waving

continuity of libidinous water
two bald eagles feed along shore
rain means nothing to them

cold means nothing to them
fish mean everything
the birds rise from below the long bank

return to woods their wings
sated and slow gulls wobble
their wings at home in raucous

air the birds know where
they're going which may be
nowhere but they keep going

because that is what
their bodies are made to do
rain means something

to mosses they puff up
put on velvet suits and shine
like green carpet movie stars

rain means something
to mushrooms each cap
smaller than a pushpin

constellations forming
overnight the forest floor
lighting up from below

rain means something to deer
they lie down in fern meadows
under tall birches it means

nothing but cold to lobstermen
who motor out haul traps
dawn and dusk rain means something

to songbirds who clam up
when it starts and when it stops
renew their lease on songful sky

3.

thwack of the driver as it slams
sledge against stake
to anchor the weir stakes

men working on floating raft
rhythmic thunks
as they breach ocean floor

birch saplings lashed for top posts
evening the boats come
home the bay silken calm

wisps of fog drift over
brittle grass pheasant
swift robin even gulls

tuck their cold feet
under downy bellies
glide toward sleep

Dulse camps teeter on cobbled basalt
where storms have heaped a seawall
topped with tumult of silvered
wharf timbers and weir stakes
enough driftwood scrap to salvage for a shack
paint the battered door dusty blue.

A rusty slatted bed kerosene pooled
in a glass-chimney lamp waiting for a match
dirty teapot on the camp stove
it's home for a night or two
when tides are right for gathering.
Stone slips wait gray and smooth from wear

where yellow dories are winched and
skidded to motor offshore headed
for the dulsing ground. A man
who works the intertidal shore
says I can smell the tide coming in.
I raise my face to the wind to try to catch

what he knows. Cold and crystal clear
the water laps the rocks and rattles them
as it recedes. The man pulls fistsful
of purple weed off tide-bare rocks
a gentle rip sounding with each pull
the ribbons gathered in his basket

dark as iodine deep as hay scythed
and piled in ricks harvest picked by hand
gathered from the transmutation of light
that sways at high tide like hair in the wind
and lies still for combing when the tide recedes
cropland where sea and rock do the tillage.

Some say a car can pick its time
not miles or rust or sludge for oil
determines when it dies. There's will
in every drive train and when it fails
the end comes fast.

When Carly bought her camp the Chev
was glad to get off-road at last
and try the cobble of a low-tide road,
algaed stone that spends half
each day and night

immersed in Fundy tide. The Chev
would round pond's edge rattling
like a tinker's cart then lurch
up the wooded lane to camp
belly-scraping the grass

but never faltering as if it shared its owner's
joy to escape accounts, repairs
and altercations in the night. A night spent
overlooking the seawall and the pond
held within those stony arms

was better than a thousand road trips
down a superhighway, so few miles
it takes to get to a place of soulful peace.
Maybe in that blessed state of nowhere
the Chev felt some gasket

gauge or seal release. No more. It chose
the spot to give up the ghost
returning on the cobble just far enough
to pass the spot where Dark Harbour brook
refreshes the pond then

the Chev refused to move. Despite
incoming tide and earnest urging
it simply was done. No more
oil changes or tune-ups or patching up rust.
It knew itself

and gave itself, first tires then chassis
then up through windows and clear
to roof, the salt water came
with its load of primal microbial
wealth. The Chev sank

into communion with the hermits,
dulsers, dories and shacks,
the falling-down tower once used
for torching herring, gave itself
to the sea, our deepest ancestral home.

—*for Carly Fleet*

■ THE LUMINOUS MOTHER

Solitude, my mother, tell me my life again.

—O. V. DE L. MILOSZ

I light two candles of uneven height
one for my brother and one for my mother
both dead in the same inscrutable year.

After burning for two days
the candles are the same height. What
is the science of their diminishing?

I want an explanation about the matter
when I should be paying attention
to the condition of my soul.

I take Whitman's command
as my own. I do not bow to death.
I place my hand against its cheek

as the heart quiets and grows still
the face loses its glow a little blossom
of blood seeps from capillaries on a chapped lip.

Sunglow on greasewood and saguaro crowns,
a brown tinge hovers in the gaps
between mountain ridge and city

her molecules hovering today in the dirt
of city air molecules released
to dissipate—up she goes—spleen liver

brain and lymph sleeve of skin
that housed her. All gone. Up you go
old girl into the forever that made you

and now unmakes the work of 102 years
girl lonely and wonderstruck
who walked the streets of Greenwich Village.

Her mother said At your age you should
wear something beautiful and gave her
the sapphire ring but the ring

was not beautiful to the girl so she walked
to a bookstore where an old couple
called her close to show her an anemone

that had just opened. That was beautiful—
ephemeral veins of color. The mourner
must bless what is wonderful even though

he can't see it writes Leon Wieseltier
turning to prayer without belief
the Kaddish to give form and rhythm to grief

prayer that never mentions the dead
only the return to circular time
time that renews itself not time that runs out.

Say it three times a day for a year
not the funeral bonnet worn in silence
not the pyre on the Ganges not

brain through the nostrils on the Nile.
The sacred begins at the tip of the tongue.
Say it. Magnified and sanctified.

I leave her gaudy plastic necklaces
at the Shrine of the Luminous Mother—
fake turquoise flecked with fake silver

white pop-pearls and a strand of shells.
They join milagros and rosaries
photos of other people's people

the dead fading into sepia in the punishing
desert sun. The first time I visited the shrine
my mother nearby in St. Mary's Hospice

where she could feel "this thing"
moving like an animal
burrowing into her insides

I found an Inca dove trapped
behind the altar's Plexiglas doors
the bird panicking and beating its wings

against the clear wall. I wondered
for a moment was it supposed to be in there
with the wilted chrysanthemums,

prayer candles and folded notes to the lost.
An offering? I thought of Darwin's account—
birds deprived of freedom to migrate

in anguish tearing feathers from their breasts
and I set the bird free. I thought of northern woods
and the labor of clearing a trail removing the obstacles—

deadfalls alder scrub and hardhack—
that had hindered my entrance
into forested tangle where all stages

of living and dying are revealed
mushrooms imagining themselves
and emerging along a seam of decay

the fallen fir with its starburst of naked limbs
circling out from the trunk the bog woods
where a stream made luminous brown with peat tannins

runs through hummocks of wild grass and tamarack saplings
where a rill over basalt cobble riles foam in the water
and how that reminded my friend who walked with me there

of a time he'd gone as a boy to Fenway Park
and in the men's room saw foam
in the big collective urinal and thought it must be sperm.

I went to the woods to pray with my hands
after grief had flattened me
and I could not swallow the losses.

I've looked down on people for their brokenness
and I've looked down on myself for my brokenness.
Now I see this is where love comes from

that death compels us to love. I never loved my mother
my mother confessed to me near the end. I know
I was supposed to but I couldn't. But you took her in

she lived with us throughout my childhood.
I had no choice. You had a choice. You took her in.
You might not have felt love but you acted with love.

My hand on top of her head. White hair
thin as her skin too had become. Vain till
the end that her hair be right—parted

above the left eyebrow combed to the right
then a few wispy bangs pulled to forehead
sides brushed back over ears. Frail hand

mimicking the motions of grooming
as I enact them. Face pursing up as she would
at her dressing table putting on her face

each morning and taking it off
each night witnessing herself
become who she saw herself to be.

Usually at about this time the nurse says
we ask if they're ready if you're ready.
Stopping the oxygen. The desert outside

the window so white. It looks like snow
she said. The hospice doc
had kneeled beside her bed eye level.

Is it all right if I ask you anything at all?
Of course. What do you think happens
when we die? Nothing. Blackness.

I don't think there's anything else.
White of clouds carnations cotton blankets.
White of hair and white of imagined snow

and white of pillows all around to brace her.
White of her last request. Ice cream
her last words. What flavor? friends joked

feeling in the request some *joie de vivre*
a bit of her flair remaining.
But this was no pleasure. She had thrush.

Her system had stopped fighting invaders.
Her mouth on fire her throat her lips.
Her hands folded like little cat paws

under her chin. I can't talk she mouthed.
Voice of air. That's okay. I can just sit with you.
Starting the morphine. Brain starting to slip

and she lies still. How long? I ask.
Doc says could be a week.
Like this? It is her outrage that speaks in me

and she hears it from her liminal place.
Her breathing shifts defiant and self-possessed
she chooses no and slides away

into silence. Why does it come to me
the memory of my right hand on her carotid
as the rhythm slowed gentled went still?

Dear Mother forgive me my fear and anger
my failure to bridge the unspoken
the chasm of what was and was not possible

between two people bound by blood and love
which here I speak
though still it will elude me forever

your cruelty invisible to you
as mine must be to me
though in this last test of our caring

we have not failed. Let it stop here
at least some quantum
of our aggrieved silence. "The blind

are required to bless the moon."
From what sacred text
do these words come? From this one.

"What solace is there in silence?"

Night in Vermont under the maples.
Drinking beer on the porch. Wicker chairs.
I've spent the day driving back roads
through hills that harbored me in my poverty
but conversation led to Cambodia, a refugee
who'd run the narrow path through jungle,
mine field, riven bodies. This is fun,
the eight-year-old laughed,
water to his chin, mother, father,
four kids wading through rice paddy
in the dark. Father knew the route
from nights smuggling from Thailand
blocks of ice balanced on his shoulders.
Whatever it took he did. Kept a little
flake of gold under the base of an oil lamp.
Keep this in case I don't return.
Four nights on the run, four days hiding in weeds,
four years in refugee camp learning English
until the American saw them in a brochure,
photo of the whole family posed holding
their number, and liked the way they looked.

Night in Vermont under the maples.
Drinking beer. Wicker chairs.
The sculptor taps the cheap rattan table
and laughs. His staff of fifteen
in Phnom Penh is splitting bamboo
and washing it in the Mekong. He's fashioned
two gigantic lungs, joined two gigantic stomachs,
structures made of plants latticed and tied,
later, grids from rice sacks, soil pigment, beeswax,

nothing but air in their middles and
even their skins, shapes for something
just coming to, tentative and light,
though he has learned to boil the fibers
in a drum with oil to make them strong.

Night in Vermont. Drinking beer
on the porch. I had trouble finding the house
where I'd lived those decades ago
so many more dirt roads vining
through the woods than I remembered.
Witchcat Road. Livestock trailer
hitched to pickup blocking the way.
Cold Hollow Range above, a billow
of deciduous calm. Whatever story
I'd hoped to find was gone. Instead
young couple coaxing heifers,
a clumsy job of loading them,
the animals confused and climbing
on each other's backs as they crowded in,
steel drumming with their hooves.

The couple wore matched t-shirts.
Farmer Brown. Local Harvest. URL.
Grass fed, managed grazing, meat and eggs
in harmony with Earth. Order online
for pickup or delivery, the form
and practice of a family, four kids
and "Name the red calf," that wants
to introduce you to its land.
Theirs was not the story I'd tried
to make of my removal to these hills
when an angel-headed hipster wrote me
a note saying, Revolution means

move to a farm, and I did,
four-year-old daughter and me
barely twenty-two, working
as dishwasher at ski resort.

One Toggenburg milk goat,
handful of barred rock hens,
freezer full of green beans and
home-pressed cider, hoeing into
witchgrass that hated to yield.
Wood heat and cold cold cold through the
crystalline winter nights of the North.
But I was tough and thought the pastoral
meant going back to find something lost,
Franklin County then more desperate than I was
dairy farms dilapidated and failing
which must have lightened the sense
of my failure or else spurred resistance to it.
When my old VW blew its head gasket
I told the welfare case-worker
(what blue-blood New Englander
sits in that chair without shame?)
if they bought me a car I'd get another job.

Night in Vermont under the maples.
Drinking beer on the porch. Wicker chairs.
The story I need isn't in the past
but one in which stories converge,
the intuition for getting out
from under what oppresses you
a force as clear as fission or mitosis.
War and poverty, denial and greed
are forms of human-made
winter from which the world

is perpetually trying to recover.
Tolstoy said (I read this in
Hayden Carruth's "California")
the purpose of poetry
is to "infect" the world
with feeling and so
induce a change of conscience
a change in care for the injured and poor.

After the heifers were loaded,
Farmer Brown pulled the truck aside
and waved me on. Thanks for waiting.
No problem. There's a white calf
over there by the side of road.
Simple fact, slight smile, averted gaze.
I slowed, rolled down the window,
eyes narrowing on knee-high weeds.
The white calf lay curled and trembling
in its grassy enclosure, trying
to make itself invisible by finding
a place from which it could not see.
What are you doing there, little one,
all by yourself? I tried to make my voice
a shelter and invitation before I passed.

—*for Sopheap Pich*

Then the news says again that hate
has made death bigger so big
you don't want to find words
nine black citizens shot in bible study
by a white man enflamed by
ranters and haters, guns for fun
and profit, traitors
padlocking allegiance to slavery
onto the state capitol dome.

You've found it hard enough
to say what one or two deaths
have meant to you and how
your own death has been a constant
companion, gentling over the decades
so now you can hear it whisper
not yet, not yet, but soon, be in love
with the day, learn to cultivate
artemisia, aquilegia, horsemint, rue

but do not turn to flower beds
to understand the woe of knowing
the souls who lived inside these names
Pinckney Simmons Hurd
Singleton Thompson Sanders
Middleton-Doctor Jackson Lance.
Turn to flower beds to woo the ground
on which the monstrous grief has fallen
grief that the faithful pray will leaven burdened soil.

What is a day to the astronaut
floating two hundred miles
above Earth the space station
whirling fifteen and a half times
a day around the planet while
he drifts weightless as if unmoving
sipping meals from a plastic pouch?
Is that how it works keeping
everything contained
against the drift? His twin is
down there donating biometrics
to the database. What is a year
to them, their bones and hearts
and brains? That's what the
instruments want to know
or what we've taught them
to want. The space twin will
pay the higher price for his
unearthly habitation. Bodies
need gravity or some system
that simulates the magnetic pull
of mantle and core. He can see
home from a porthole in space
the planet from out here
sublime a blue and white
ball so tender it might be
made of glass just forming
at the tip of the glassblower's rod.

The Earth twin watches his brother
lift from the Cosmodrome.
Zero to seventeen thousand

in twelve minutes. "It feels like
the hand of God has come down
and grabbed you by the collar
and ripped you off the planet.
You know you're either going
to float in space or you're going
to be dead." What is Earth
to the astronaut? The exception
to emptiness. Boatloads of planets
lie further in the black concealment
of space. Best that we don't know
their voraciousness and need.
Our home we know is troubled
yet still in the heyday
of its experiment with life.
Thanks cyanobacteria
for your evolutionary largesse
the Great Oxygenation Event
that made us possible.

I'm writing this to find my way
into the fray over fracking—
wild card as it seems now that
I've gone so far out into space.
No one wants to hear again
about flaming water faucets
exploited towns and farms
heartland riddled with quakes
water poisoned and stuck back
in the ground to find its way home.
Space might be the only way
to see what kind of sky we need
and how the Great Carbonation Event
might be flipping the way
Earth does or doesn't do life.

We say "blue marble" we say
"Mother Earth" we say "home."
The astronaut says "Beautiful."
Earth from space says "Keep me."
The only thing that matters is
the carbon, so homeland
security means leave it
in the ground. Lock it up
with soldiers standing guard.
Shelter it with grassland and trees.

—for Taylor Brorby

My friend a writer and scientist
has retreated to a monastery
where he has submitted himself
out of exhaustion to not knowing.
He's been thinking about
the incarnation a.k.a. Big Bang
after hearing a monk's teaching
that crucifixion was not the hard part
for Christ. Incarnation was.
How to squeeze all of that
all-of-that into a body. I woke
that Easter to think of the Yaqui
celebrations taking place in our city
the culminating ritual of the Gloria
when the disruptive spirits
with their clacking daggers and swords
are repelled from the sanctuary
by women and children
throwing cottonwood leaves and confetti
and then my mother rose
in me rose from the anguish
of her hospice bed a woman
who expected to direct all the action
complaining to her nurse
I've been here three days
and I'm not dead yet—not ready
at one hundred and two to give up
control even to giving up control.
I helped with the morphine clicker.
Peace peace peace the stilling
at her throat the hazel eye
become a glassy marble. Yet here she is

an Easter irreverent still rising
to dress in loud pastels
and turn me loose
in Connecticut woods to hunt
my basket of marshmallow eggs
jelly beans and chocolate rabbit
these fakeries of nature made vestal
incarnated in their nest of shiny manufactured grass.

—*for Brother Coyote*

These are the synergetic rules that evolution is employing and
trying to make clear to us. . . .

—BUCKMINSTER FULLER

I.

MORNING IN THE LUNG

Link by link the rusted
    chain
releases as morning
    begins
to warm the enclosure
    where
psychotria, ficus and
    euphorbiaceae
transpire. The experimental
    world shimmers
under glass, the space frame
    white as starlight
the glass mottled with what
    rain
the prolonged drought
    will allow
in our desert out there
    but in here . . .
clanking links
    of rusted chain
release, adjusting atmospheric
    pressure
that rises and falls
    with the sun

three acres of manufacture
    oh little planet
of ingenuity and audacious hope
    where the botanist
spends nine months
    keying
and counting and naming each
    plant
in the tropical forest
    where
the sandbox tree disperses
    seed
by exploding fruit
    into space
where the marine biologist
    seeds 10,000
red hermits into the diminutive
    ocean
to eat invasive
    brown algae.
Oh little planet . . .
    clack clack
the experiment breathes and drips
    and disperses
data into the throat of
    the future.
Link by link this
    organ
becomes organism
    no artifice
hidden: complexity
    underpinning
and overriding
    the random.

Clack clack . . .
   the diaphragm
rises link by link
   the building
listens to itself
   breathe.

2.

It failed of course though
the idea was that if
we screw up Earth

we can live elsewhere in pods
and this would be the test
ground patent protected

innovation as a gamble
built on three acres of
stainless steel protection

from microbes beneath
and a hundred-year
business plan—to Mars by 1990!

Okay. Never mind. Let's just
try to get enough oxygen
to keep the team alive.

3.

LANDSCAPE EVOLUTION OBSERVATORY

The story of human care has not yet come to an end.
—ROBERT POGUE HARRISON, GARDENS

Nothing to look at
    in what once was farm

Now basement with tubs named
    scrap case
    bulkhead fittings
    terminal blocks

Drawers named
    tape   electrical   solder
    pliers   cutters   crimpers
    hex wrench   driver bit

Carton called
    Cables To Go

Steel I-beams and cross struts
    painted
    Praying Mantis Green

Roaring fans fill
    every span
    of techno
    sphere

Keep It Moving seems
    prime rule
    of Earth
    design

Sloping garden plots
    arrayed with black
    volcanic soil

delivery streamed on live cam
    work crew
    sweating through the night
    to lay the beds

now scored with plastic cups
    5.1 and 5.2
    6.3 and 7.4
    in rows
    and columns

seedlings set
    three hundred strong
    lined up like
    terracotta warriors

eighteen hundred sensors
    buried
    in the soil
    tubing
    misters

footprints Nike-stamped
    into inert soil
    between the rows

no fleecy cotton bolls

no viney peas

it's early in the growing season
    syringes mounted
    on a panel
    clear tubules
    twining up

to do some calibrated work
    tiny sample bottles
    crated in their little
    cardboard slots

"lysimeters" penciled on the box
    whatever that means
    someone wants
    to be sure
    to get it right

A philosopher might say these
    tools and tubes and gustless
    ceaseless indoor winds
    express the vocation of care

liquid nails
    eucolastic one   gun grade
    wash cloth caked with caulk

Let's not get stuck
    in grieving
    the lost wild

Let's
    domesticate
    space

What does it take
    to make it all happen again?
    What all?

The firestorm that lit our planet
    into its condition
    of shook-foil joy.

Read:
    Hopkins

Read:
    Camus
    "The sun taught me that history is not everything."

Read:
    exoplanet
    space colony
    afterEarth
    vivarium
    in the hollow
    of an asteroid

Carton called
    Copy Paper

Bucket called
    Let's Do This
    replacing
    an empty can of glue.

4.

HUMAN HABITAT

Some did not want to alter the design
when the failure message
said massive problem with oxygen.
Some wanted to live full tilt with risk.

By then we were too weak for daily chores:
feeding chickens, hoeing yams,
calibrating pH this and N_2 that
felt like climbing Everest.

We didn't expect the honeybees
to die. Glass blocked the long-wave
light that guides them.
Farm soil too rich in microbes

concrete too fresh ate the oxygen.
We had pressure problems,
recalibrating the sniffer. Bone tired
I reread Aristotle by waning light.

Being is either actual or potential.
The actual is prior to substance.
Man prior to boy, human prior to seed,
Hermes prior to chisel hitting wood.

I leafed through *Turner's England*,
left the book open at Stonehenge.
A shepherd struck by lightning lies dead,
dog howling, several sheep down too.

The painter gave gigantic proportion
to sulphurous god-rimmed clouds
lightning slashing indigo sky
while close at hand lie fallen stones

dead religion, pages dusty
brown leaf shards gathering
in the gutter yet I cannot turn the page
wondering what I am and when

in the story of life my life is taking place.
Now what? No shepherd. No cathedral.
How is it then that I read love
in pages that lie open before me?

5.

TROPICALITY

If I had given birth to seventeen children
and five had died at birth, another two from pox
or war, would I then have loved the ten
any less? So too the world comes to us unlocked

without protection, the forest deprived of forest,
air handlers roaring in place of panther,
no monkey, mole or passerine to nest
among the waxy leaves and anthers.

No weather in the ecosphere glassed
inside itself though drops of rain descend
to stain the page, water that's passed
through leaves and kidneys and will again

assent to laws of intermolecular
attraction: water flows against the down-
ward tug of gravity, a force suggesting cellular
intellect, xylem pulling liquid to the crown.

What does a forest want? Soil to be turned
by worms, cavities to enter or be entered,
honey honey everywhere, and sometimes to be burned,
maniacal song at dawn and dusk, the dead to be interred,

blue morpho nectaring, long tongue of bat
slipped into orchid well, long breath of trades
tumbled in from the sea. But we're a long way from that.
Can someone please turn up the rain?

Time to narrow parameters: what do plants do
to adapt to duress? Some speckled eye,
some speckled egg, some speckled light
and chemistry set will fracture open the way.

.

6.

FOG DESERT

Snowfall comes from a woman who
asks what's that plant that looks like a
Christmas tree. Agave, I say.
She can't believe it, so phallic,
the bloom atop the bladed globe.
It dies after it blooms, I say.
Navajo kid, black concert tee,
grins then writes, Death. Hands it to me.

Thanks for the word, man, I say, when
I meet him exiting the tour.
Yeah, I figured a poet could
use that. His bottom lip pierced with
two obsidian rings. His wife
too. Body mod, the earliest
art, clay beads, ochre chests, hawk moth
pupae strapped to calves for dancing.

Theory of art: let there be no
artifice, only enactment
like agave having its day.
History is boring and dead.
Art, the day aroused, the practice
of thrill and caw and cry and chill,
a child obsessed with aurochs, flood
receding, damage done and yet . . .

7.

OCEAN

The ocean has not been so quiet for a long while. . . .
—ROBINSON JEFFERS, "EVENING EBB"

I lost my paddle blade   rowing the plastic boat
into the artificial sea   PVC pipe worked
enough to land me   moor the boat
what rough beast   is put to rest
the wave machine   lulling with cadenced beats
no squid, herring, dolphin   racing in the Mother sea
backtrack to elemental   obfuscating evanescence
driven by wind and turning   mollusk house and mangrove stilt
while visitors   gaze from catwalk
at me a specimen   with notebook
sitting on concrete rock   on shell midden shore
and here we see a human type   defining characteristics:
solitude, hypergraphia   staring into space
the visitor takes one more picture   before moving to savannah
all adaptations to time and place   each performing
as I do the thing that I am   like any captive being
defined by constraints   oh sacred breath

8.

EVENING IN THE LUNG

For to have breath is to be sacred
For to be sacred is to repeat like rain
For to repeat like rain is to fall as if purely
For to fall as if purely is to carry the dirt
For to carry the dirt is to be pharmaceutical
For to be pharmaceutical is to control birth, death, darkness and pain
For to control birth, death, darkness and pain is human privilege
For human privilege is to imagine the rain as cleansing
For to imagine the rain as cleansing is to fall in love with the weather
For to fall in love with the weather is to accept the day
For to accept the day is to remember the future
For to remember the future is to reverse time
For to reverse time is to outlive death
For to outlive death is the cry that everything is crying
For the cry that everything is crying is to build capacity
For to build capacity is what people say about work
For what people say about work is not apocalypse
For what is not apocalypse is invention
For invention is the brainless beauty of Earth

Say yes to the pomegranate because
the pomegranate said yes to the desert
yes to Afghanistan and Sonora
yes to Pima and O'odham
yes to Father Kino's gunnysack
packed with quince, peach and pear
crossing perilous ocean east
following learned rivers north.

A river learns the land while carving
its way as fruit learns its sweetness
from enduring seclusion crammed
in dense and lightless ground.
The pomegranate made no complaint
of its hardship above ground or below
yes to aridity yes to monsoon
yes to backyard yes to industrial orchard.

Persephone and Eve knew pomegranates.
What color were the arils that they
pulled from the mottled leathery skin?
Blood red if history were to tell
the truth. But in the Mission Garden
and in a thousand backyards lost
among weeds stands the tree growing
yes to kitchen yes to dining table.

Wait for it to ripen then slice off
the top and bottom. Open the cask
of the fruit and find black seeds and flesh
so bright and wet they look like

frogs' eggs in a pond. But no
each seed is portioned in its leathery room
each cluster nested in protected space
this golden fruit that is the yes defying history.

—*for Adela Licona*

After you died I took you for a drive
across northern New England
refusing to leave you
to the violence of your death.
I took the river and lakes route
following the sinuous Androscoggin
and slipping between vitreous
ponds, Bach sonatas setting the mood,
the harpsichord trilling like thrush song
viola reaching into the dark register
of feeling that crossed three centuries
to be with us, that miracle of art's
timelessness. I don't want to
imagine the moment of impact
though here it is refusing to depart.
I'll counter it with water
and picture you slipping under,
your wild hair waving like rockweed
in the salty slosh, your eyes opened
to the benthic marvel of deep sea
creatures no human has ever seen,
the seahorses ponying up to watch you
float among them, the bioluminescent
swimmers of the lightless zones
coming close to illuminate the way,
bluefish swimming back and forth
bragging to you of their color palette,
the all-embracing water of our origin
and its inventive power, molecules
that danced as mountain snows, churned
in spring down rocky forest streams,

sprawled into the languorous ecstasy of rivers
then found a delta where they dispersed
into the moon slung sea you loved,
your mind and body one with them now.

—*in memory of Rafe Sagarin*

■ DEATH VALLEY SEQUENCE

The future enters us, in order to transform
itself in us, long before it happens.

—RAINER MARIA RILKE

I.

Forget what you think you know
about beauty and what lasts.
These forsaken hills and salt flats
erosion dune encrustation
are ghosts of a lake a storm a savannah
all here and gone like the stars
that blew apart to make
the complicated molecules
here now organized and named
Funeral Hills and Eureka Valley
Dante's View and Zabriskie Point
a vast space where the land
can think about itself
without distractions
perfect in its desolation
and yet full of the long story
of invention that has been spilling
out of space the dull force
that has been pulling the valley apart
the blazing heat that has purified
the air and made the past lie down to rest
the future wait for a moment before descending.

2.

Black ribbon of asphalt unspools
through the Amargosa Chaos
as you leave the dull glow
of towns forgotten when
mines shut down and you
descend through chalk hills
stained with iron red bands
terrain gutted and gullied by time
a place where migrant and miner
picked their way through rock
made tea from twigs
forced water to rise in a dry pit
they came to call a well
and marked with stovepipe
their lost voices distant
as the bells that hung
on a mine mule's harness
echoing long the tasks
once necessary in the world's
machinery then lost. The place
opens a rift in you right down
to the fossil bed of your cells.

3.

We did not have flowers
we did not have water
or sky except the night's
version this "we" that is
the planet speaking for
its multiple personalities
all we have been
since the dust gathered
into a ball and the ball
heated into a furnace
that cooked up life.
Some say the first cells
boiled out of vents
on the floor of the sea
black smokers that spilled
energy eager to make more
of itself. But even that came late.
For a billion years we were
a hot rock without a sea.
Water kept drifting into space
without an atmosphere to hold it.
We were volcanoes. We became a sea.

4.

We were volcanoes
spewing molten rock
and gas that rose
and hovered until
it came to form
a shield around
the cooling Earth.
Some of the gas
became rain that
fell back to ground
and pooled. Comets
and asteroids crashed
with their drops of
melting ice. A billion
years or so of that
and we grew into
something more
than barren rock
land and sky falling
into relationship
a cycle of reciprocating
moves. We became a sea.

5.

Hoodoo badland turtleback
a place this stark needs
its own vocabulary
unverdant land
testing life for extremes
that lie ahead as deserts spread
and water goes and sky
has nothing good to say
about the future. Hard to stay
in the moment when time
has gouged and layered
its story out so frankly
siltstone sandstone mudstone
like neighbors that can't stop
talking about the past
and all they've been through.
If only I could get the sequence
of events right . . . what?
It seems I'd know a continuity
that could stand up to death
mountain flanks taking snow
and turning it into wildflowers.

6.

Bear poppy
Gravel ghost
Saucer plant
Napkin ring buckwheat
Desert rue
Fishhook cactus
Grape soda lupine
Parish larkspur
Desert trumpet
Beavertail cactus
Bladder sage
Cheesebush
Winter fat
Brittlebush
Pricklepoppy
Prince's plume
Devil's Cornfield
Mormon tea
Rattlesnake weed
Rocknettle
Ravens settling
into salt cedars

7.

Every name
a location on
the map of lonely
visitors. While
some tribes who
stayed in place
gave names
that were verbs.
Nothing was a thing
itself and everything
was busy being
itself. No word for
"desert rue" rather
"to be the desert rue"
so the whole landscape
spun with states of being
the land not "the land"
to be bought and quartered
but "to be the land"
as if made sentient just
by being here. "Valley of Life"
they called the place.

8.

Land this impoverished and vast
could be another planet
not Earth with its celebrity glow
of blue ocean and green terrain.
Salt stain leaks across the flats
dirt flow and rubble seam out
from the Panamints into alluvial fans
and the Funeral Mountains
rumple like the ruched black silk
of Victorian mourning.
Heartless and sere the desert
does not nurture the complacent.
Whatever lives here has learned
the kangaroo rat to live without water
the coyote melon to let
its above ground parts die.
Rock bent and rebent, slopes
jarred with fault and slippage
force of the planet's slow flex
and strain the valley rent in two
as underlying plates grind past each other.
How perfect the illusion of stillness.

9.

Sometimes it seems
as if time is the material
of which we're made.
Grain by grain we add up
like sand ground down
to gritty beads
by an archaic sea.
Chalk hills built up
grain by grain
from crushed mollusks
and crustaceans. How many
clam shells does it take
to build an acropolis?
Ridge after ridge lined up
like dancers in reciprocating
gesture flirting with embrace
but keeping their distance
posed at just so intervals
as if choreographed
into pattern and form
though it is the eye
that choreographs.

10.

Why did we come here
poet and astronomer
out for a walk
at the end of the world?
In Titus Canyon
we saw rock walls
that told so many
stories of the violent
past it was impossible
to parse them though
water had done its part
to rip open this cleavage
in stone. Sparse
creosote bloomed at the summit
paltry yellow stars sparkling
on desiccated stems.
Easy to read Death Valley
as a cautionary tale
barrenness and heat
left in the wake
of human passing. We came
for the clarity of desert light.

11.

Some scientists say
it was inevitable that
the universe would make
beings able to comprehend
the cosmic story and that
we'd keep looking into
the dark energy
of what we don't know
for something
we perceive that isn't.
It was never enough for us
just to survive. We had to
make something of ourselves
give something back of ourselves
register our inner lives
in the record of what is.
We are not just made
of the same material
as stars but of the same
self-ordering force that thinks
it can do something about entropy.
The universe aglitter in the salt pan.

12.

A gust of wind picks up
blows dust aswirl
from Furnace Creek
southeast toward
Badwater Basin.
Winds here make
the Eureka Dunes
sing in a groaning chant
like cloistered monks.
The thicker the sand
the lower the note
dune crusts collapsing
and flowing downhill
the mountain of sand
their amplifier. Some days
it is so quiet a person
strains for sound
and feels lucky to catch
the whooo-ing of a breeze.
Some days the valley
is as quiet as death
until the canyon wren disrupts
eternity with a moment of song.

—*for Stephen Strom*

ACKNOWLEDGMENTS

I am grateful to the Hermitage Artist Retreat in Englewood, Florida, and the Vermont Studio Center in Johnson, Vermont, for time and refuge to complete this work. Thanks also to Eric Magrane and all the good people at Biosphere 2 who invited me to participate in the Poetic Field Research Performance Weekend. Thanks to photographer and astronomer Stephen Strom, who invited me to travel with him to Death Valley National Park for work on the poem sequence that appears here and in his collection of photographs *Death Valley: Painted Light* (George F. Thompson).

My gratitude to friends and colleagues for their insight and inspiration—Chris Cokinos, Joshua Marie Wilkinson, Susan Briante, Farid Matuk, Aurelie Sheehan, Ander Monson, Adela Licona, Tyler Meier, Diana Liverman, Lee Medovoi, Kathleen Dean Moore, Robin Kimmerer, Katherine Coles, Scott Russell Sanders, Barbara Hurd, Scott Slovic, Peter Cunningham, Ara Fitzgerald, Peter Hoffman, Carly Fleet, Gary Paul Nabhan, Alan Weisman, Beckie Kravitz, Mitchell Thomashow, and William Fox—and, always, to my gifted daughter, Lucinda Bliss. Gratitude in memoriam to the unforgettable Rafe Sagarin. Thank you to the University of Arizona, College of Social and Behavioral Sciences, for appointing me Agnese Nelms Haury Chair of Environment and Social Justice.

Boundless gratitude to the John Simon Guggenheim Memorial Foundation for a 2015 fellowship and to my editor, Paul Slovak, for his support of this work.

Grateful acknowledgment to the editors of these journals and other venues that have published the following poems, often in earlier versions:

Academy of American Poets, Poem-a-Day: "Human Habitat," "Stairway to Heaven"

American Scientist: "Mosquitoes"

Cutthroat: "Primordial Soup," "Reading Palms," "The Toothbrush"

Green Linden Press: "Castalia"

The Huffington Post, 7 Rings: An Artist's Game of Telephone: "The Mirror"

The Massachusetts Review: "The Drowned Man," "Provincetown"

Orion: "Chauvet"

Poetry Northwest: "Some Bugs"

Shenandoah blog: "Afterlife"

Spiral Orb: "Questions for a Saguaro," "What the Desert Is Thinking," written for the Poetic Inventory of the Sonoran Desert Project

Talking River: "Dark Harbour," "In Praise of a Nameless Place," "The International Motel"

Terrain.org: "Chauvet," "Morning in the Lung"

Zócalo: "All Souls"

"Cartoon" was written for the *Golden Shovel Anthology*, edited by Peter Kahn in honor of Gwendolyn Brooks, forthcoming from the University of Arkansas Press.

"Chauvet" was printed as a limited-edition broadside by Juniper White to benefit the online journal *terrain.org*.

"Death Valley Sequence" appears in *Death Valley: Painted Light*, photographs by Stephen Strom, published by the University of Arizona Press.

"Golden Pomegranate" was written for Adela Licona in response to her photographs, the collaboration appearing in *Edible Baja Arizona*.

"Homeland Security" was written for Taylor Brorby's anthology *Fracture: Essays, Poems, and Stories on Fracking in America*, from Ice Cube Press. Thanks to twin astronauts Mark and Scott Kelly, suggested in the poem, for their inspiration and courage.

"Questions for a Saguaro" and "What the Desert Is Thinking" appear in *The Sonoran Desert: A Literary Field Guide*, from the University of Arizona Press.

"Rillito" was written in celebration of Bat Night in Tucson and appeared in *Groundwater: The Art, Design and Science of a Dry River*, published by the Confluencenter at the University of Arizona.

ABOUT THE AUTHOR

Alison Hawthorne Deming's most recent books are *Zoologies: On Animals and the Human Spirit* (Milkweed, 2014) and *Death Valley: Painted Light*, a collaboration with photographer Stephen Strom (George F. Thompson, 2016). She is the author of three additional nonfiction books and four previous poetry books, including *Science and Other Poems*, winner of the Walt Whitman Award. Her work has won fellowships from the National Endowment for the Arts and the Fine Arts Work Center; the Stegner Fellowship from Stanford University; and the Bayer Award in Science Writing. Former director of the University of Arizona Poetry Center and a 2015 Guggenheim Fellow, Deming is Agnese Nelms Haury Chair in Environment and Social Justice and a professor in creative writing at the University of Arizona. She lives in Tucson and on Grand Manan Island in New Brunswick, Canada.

JOHN ASHBERY
Selected Poems
Self-Portrait in a Convex
  Mirror

PAUL BEATTY
Joker, Joker, Deuce

JOSHUA BENNETT
The Sobbing School

TED BERRIGAN
The Sonnets

LAUREN BERRY
The Lifting Dress

PHILIP BOOTH
Lifelines: Selected Poems
  1950–1999

JULIANNE BUCHSBAUM
The Apothecary's Heir

JIM CARROLL
Fear of Dreaming:
  The Selected Poems
Living at the Movies
Void of Course

ALISON HAWTHORNE DEMING
Genius Loci
Rope
Stairway to Heaven

CARL DENNIS
Another Reason
Callings
New and Selected Poems
  1974–2004
Practical Gods
Ranking the Wishes
Unknown Friends

DIANE DI PRIMA
Loba

STUART DISCHELL
Dig Safe

STEPHEN DOBYNS
Velocities: New and Selected
  Poems: 1966–1992

EDWARD DORN
Way More West

ROGER FANNING
The Middle Ages

ADAM FOULDS
The Broken Word

CARRIE FOUNTAIN
Burn Lake
Instant Winner

AMY GERSTLER
Crown of Weeds
Dearest Creature
Ghost Girl
Medicine
Nerve Storm
Scattered at Sea

EUGENE GLORIA
Drivers at the Short-Time Motel
Hoodlum Birds
My Favorite Warlord

DEBORA GREGER
By Herself
Desert Fathers, Uranium Daughters
God
Men, Women, and Ghosts
Western Art

TERRANCE HAYES
Hip Logic
How to Be Drawn
Lighthead
Wind in a Box

NATHAN HOKS
The Narrow Circle

ROBERT HUNTER
Sentinel and Other Poems

MARY KARR
Viper Rum

JACK KEROUAC
Book of Blues
Book of Haikus
Book of Sketches

JOANNA KLINK
Circadian
Excerpts from a Secret Prophecy
Raptus

JOANNE KYGER
As Ever: Selected Poems

ANN LAUTERBACH
Hum
If in Time: Selected Poems,
  1975–2000
On a Stair
Or to Begin Again
Under the Sign

CORINNE LEE
Plenty

PHILLIS LEVIN
May Day
Mercury
Mr. Memory & Other Poems

PATRICIA LOCKWOOD
Motherland Fatherland
  Homelandsexuals

WILLIAM LOGAN
Macbeth in Venice
Madame X
Strange Flesh
The Whispering Gallery

ADRIAN MATEJKA
The Big Smoke
Mixology

MICHAEL MCCLURE
Huge Dreams: San Francisco
  and Beat Poems

ROSE MCLARNEY
Its Day Being Gone

DAVID MELTZER
David's Copy: The Selected
  Poems of David Meltzer

ROBERT MORGAN
Dark Energy
Terroir

CAROL MUSKE-DUKES
An Octave above Thunder
Red Trousseau
Twin Cities

ALICE NOTLEY
Certain Magical Acts
Culture of One
The Descent of Alette
Disobedience
In the Pines
Mysteries of Small Houses

WILLIE PERDOMO
The Essential Hits of Shorty
  Bon Bon

LIA PURPURA
It Shouldn't Have Been Beautiful

LAWRENCE RAAB
The History of Forgetting
Visible Signs: New and Selected
  Poems

BARBARA RAS
The Last Skin
One Hidden Stuff

MICHAEL ROBBINS
Alien vs. Predator
The Second Sex

PATTIANN ROGERS
Generations
Holy Heathen Rhapsody
Wayfare

ROBYN SCHIFF
A Woman of Property

WILLIAM STOBB
Absentia
Nervous Systems

TRYFON TOLIDES
An Almost Pure Empty Walking

SARAH VAP
Viability

ANNE WALDMAN
Gossamurmur
Kill or Cure
Manatee/Humanity
Structure of the World
  Compared to a Bubble

JAMES WELCH
Riding the Earthboy 40

PHILIP WHALEN
Overtime: Selected Poems

ROBERT WRIGLEY
Anatomy of Melancholy and
  Other Poems
Beautiful Country
Earthly Meditations: New and
  Selected Poems
Lives of the Animals
Reign of Snakes

MARK YAKICH
The Importance of Peeling
  Potatoes in Ukraine
Unrelated Individuals Forming a
  Group Waiting to Cross